D1178385

Parasites of Heaven

Leonard Cohen

McCLELLAND
AND STEWART
LIMITED
Toronto / Montreal

© 1966 by Leonard Cohen

ALL RIGHTS RESERVED

The Canadian Publishers

McClelland and Stewart Limited
25 Hollinger Road, Toronto 16

PRINTED AND BOUND IN CANADA

For Irving Layton

ALSO
BY
Leonard Cohen

POEMS

Let Us Compare Mythologies (1956, 1966)
The Spice-Box of Earth (1961)
Flowers for Hitler (1964)
Parasites   (1966)

NOVELS

The Favourite Game (1963)
Beautiful Losers (1966)

CONTENTS

Parasites of
Heaven

So you're the kind of vegetarian
that only eats roses
Is that what you mean
with your Beautiful Losers
1965

It's not so hard to say goodbye. True, the mind bleeds a little, but if you don't part your hair too deep nobody will mention it. And true, the ego aches like a tooth with sugar in it when it accepts at long last an alien perfection, but still the goodbyes will be made, and not from such a long way off as you thought. We're only over here, climbing the shining reflection of the rickety ladder that gave way under you, our boots snapping through the rungs with the sound of a machine gun. Look! that's a smile on the skull. Last year we thought that only hypocrites did that to their mouths.

The nightmares do not suddenly
develop happy endings
          I merely step out of them
as a five year old scientist
leaves the room
where he has disected an alarm clock

Love wears out
like overused mirrors unsilvering
          and parts of your faces
make room for the wall behind
If terror needs my round green eyes
for a masterpiece
          let it lure them with nude key-holes
mounted on an egg

And should Love decide
I am not the one
          to stand scratching his head
wondering what wall to lean on
          send King Farouk to argue
or come to me dressed as a fast

A cross didn't fall on me
when I went for hot-dogs
and the all-night Greek
slave in the Silver Gameland
didn't think I was his brother
Love me because nothing happens

I believe the rain will not
make me feel like a feather
when it comes tonight after
the streetcars have stopped
because my size is definite
Love me because nothing happens

Do you have any idea how
many movies I had to watch
before I knew surely
that I would love you
when the lights woke up
Love me because nothing happens

Here is a headline July 14
in the city of Montreal
Intervention decisive de Pearson
a la conference du Commonwealth
That was yesterday
Love me because nothing happens

Stars and stars and stars
keep it to themselves
Have you ever noticed how private
a wet tree is
a curtain of razor blades
Love me because nothing happens

Why should I be alone
if what I say is true
I confess I mean to find
a passage or forge a passport
or talk a new language
Love me because nothing happens

I confess I meant to grow
wings and lose my mind
I confess that I've
forgotten what for
Why wings and a lost mind
Love me because nothing happens

In the Bible generations pass in a paragraph, a betrayal is disposed of in a phrase, the creation of the world consumes a page. I could never pick the important dynasty out of a multitude, you must have your forehead shining to do that, or to choose out of the snarled network of daily evidence the denials and the loyalties. Who can choose what olive tree the story will need to shade its lovers, what tree out of the huge orchard will give them the particular view of branches and sky which will unleash their kisses. Only two shining people know, they go directly to the roots they lie between. For my part I describe the whole orchard.

Ah, what were the names I gave you
before I learned all names go the do-do way?
Darlin, Golden, Meadowheart

I've been walking in the far green
I've lost what all the leaves are called
Elm, Chestnut, Silver

O come here you, thou
Bring all thy, bring all thine
Far into the splinter let's sing for nothing

1958

One night I burned the house I loved,
It lit a perfect ring
In which I saw some weeds and stone
Beyond — not anything.

Certain creatures of the air
Frightened by the night,
They came to see the world again
And perished in the light.

Now I sail from sky to sky
And all the blackness sings
Against the boat that I have made
Of mutilated wings.

1960

Give me dog, dogs, wolves, to serve, praise, kneel
in thanks. Bring me torn by sin, stuffed with loot,
bring me in their wild midst, in the spiked ring
of white teeth, sharp fangs, wet mouths, cast me hard
and down. I am not food, the calf, the ewe,
I am the man to be sent to love, but
clawed first, cleansed first, taught to fight, to lose, save
my skin, my stained skin, my own old soft shell

1961

You know there was honey in my system
but I filled a honey jar
and I hid it with the moon and sun up there
It's time to be sweet again
to the poor ladies and gentlemen
Now my horoscope is starving
I've got to find that sticky jar
You can wait for signals and comets
I'm going to follow the honey flies

They aren't so bad
Some say that flies are man's best friend
Even though they tore my sleep apart
they were just doing their job
They're never wrong about the honey
That's proved by the nervous sky
and the legions dead or kicking
all along the rim of the jar

Why did I hide it so far away
Was I worried about my weight
I don't know I don't know
I didn't think anybody wanted breakfast
or I would have stayed at home
Well never mind the mornings
you tried to get the rich to love you
Put it down to love
The 11th story window is buzzing thick with flies
And listen so you'll remember
just what it was you did
That's not the Milky Way up there
that's sticky paper from your store

It's not too late for goodbyes
That's what I want to tell you all
who are waiting with indifferent expressions
between me and the honey flies
Hey there they are
sailing like a cyclone
that dips into everything you hide
They're black as hair
they rent the air
for a dollar thirty-five
They suck you through the small end of their telescope
There's no hope they say
It's our office
step inside it's a very short ride
when you're a guest of the honey flies

Nothing has been broken
      though one of the links of the chain
is a blue butterfly

Here he was attacked
      They smiled as they came and retired
baffled with blue dust

The banks so familiar with metal
      they made for the wings
The thick vaults fluttered

The pretty girls advanced
      their fingers cupped
They bled from the mouth as though struck

The jury asked for pity
      and touched and were electrocuted
by the blue antennae

A thrust at any link
      might have brought him down
but each of you aimed at the blue butterfly
1963

Here we are at the window. Great unbound sheaves of rain wandering across the mountain, parades of wind and driven silver grass. So long I've tried to give a name to freedom, today my freedom lost its name, like a student's room travelling into the morning with its lights still on. Every act has its own style of freedom, whatever that means. Now I'm commanded to think of weeds, to worship the strong weeds that grew through the night, green and wet, the white thread roots taking lottery orders from the coils of brain mud, the permeable surface of the world. Did you know that the brain developed out of a fold in the epidermis? Did you? Falling ribbons of silk, the length of rivers, cross the face of the mountain, systems of grass and cable. Freedom lost its name to the style with which things happen. The straight trees, the spools of weed, the travelling skeins of rain floating through the folds of the mountain — here we are at the window. Are you ready now? Have I dismissed myself? May I fire from the hip? Brothers, each at your window, we are the style of so much passion, we are the order of style, we are pure style called to delight a fold of the sky.

1965

When I paid the sun to run
It ran and I sat down and cried
The sun I spent my money on
Went round and round inside
The world all at once
Charged with insignificance

O love intrude into this strangerhood
Like the bloodblack river
Drive a stain of living colour
Through leper drifts of winter sleep
Silence be my wilderness
Where I can learn to master
As my heroes did
The visionary discipline
Then bear me to the shores
Of lakes we slept beside
Where I may lose with grace
The pine trees to the early mist

1959

Clean as the grass from which
the sun has burned the little dew
I come to this page
in the not so early morning
with a picture of him
whom I could not be for long
not wanting to return or begin
again the idolatry of terror

He was burned away from me
by needles by ashes
by various shames I
engineered against his innocence
by documenting the love of one
who gathered my first songs
and gave her body to my wandering

With a picture of him
grooming her thighs for a journey
with a picture of him
buying her a staring peacock feather
with a picture of him
knighted by her smile her soft fatigue
I begin the hopeless formula
she already had the gold from

Live for him huge black eyes
He never understood their purity
or how they watched him prepare
to ditch the early songs and say goodbye
Sleep beside him uncaptured darling
while I fold into a kite
the long evenings he scratched with
experiments the empty dazzling mornings
that forbid me to recall your name

With a picture of him
standing by the window while she slept
with a picture of him
wondering what adventure is
wondering what cruelty is
with a picture of him
waking her with an angry kiss
leading her body into use and time
I bargain with the fire
which must ignore the both of them

Terribly awake I wait
beside the grass your flesh pressed down.
Will you return?
What constellation will you become?

And if you live in the sky,
will I have the courage to say:
The stars have arms and mouths
and cluster round your body
like petals on the roses' throat?

Or will I bind the roots
across my head and chest
and see the stars as heaven's warts
visiting the sinner's flesh?

1957

I wonder if my brother will ever read this. He would no doubt repudiate it, gently I hope, he would say perhaps the sea is all the things you've said, dream machine, a glass eye and so forth, but even if it's true it's better left unsaid. Now I could tell him something which I never knew when I lived so close to him, that it is a luxury, this being able to leave things unsaid, a luxury enjoyed by very few. Children of the wind and water need not elaborate on what their blood knows, but how many can command this economy, how many more must scratch and paw the world in a thousand different ways just to establish the slightest connection with their true lives. Heroes and near-heroes, anointed children aimed at their waiting constellations, they may disdain to implore the horizontal world with words and organizing metaphors, but I do not have their balance, how many do, I am not aimed at anything, I am not about to ascend toward my glory, so I must blunder among my tether-ings, I must bargain for what love I'll get, outside my brief particular story no passion will unfold me, no particular has claimed me so I must indulge myself in the seedy politics of the general, and cry at gods to prove gods unreal, just as my brother and I used to cloud windowpanes with our breath so that we could draw on them with our fingers. He drew profiles for which I designed complicated eyes, and no one asks you to decide which of our efforts was the more significant.

I see you on a Greek mattress
reading the Book of Changes,
Lebanese candy in the air.
On the whitewashed wall I see
you raise another hexagram
for the same old question:
how can you be free?
I see you cleaning your pipe
with the hairpin
of somebody's innocent night.
I see the plastic Evil Eye
pinned to your underwear.
Once again you throw the pennies,
once again you read
how the pieces of the world
have changed around your question.
Did you get to the Himalayas?
Did you visit that monk in New Jersey?
I never answered any of your letters.
Oh Steve, do you remember me?

1963

Suzanne wears a leather coat.
Her legs are insured by many burnt bridges.
Her calves are full as spinnakers
in a clean race, hard from following music
beyond the maps of any audience.

Suzanne wears a leather coat
because she is not a civilian.
She never walks casually down Ste Catherine
because with every step she must redeem
the clubfoot crowds and stalk the field
of huge hail-stones that never melted,
I mean the cemetery.

Stand up! stand!
Suzanne is walking by.
She wears a leather coat. She won't stop
to bandage the fractures she walks between.
She must not stop, she must not
carry money.
Many are the workers in charity.

Few serve the lilac,
few heal with mist.
Suzanne wears a leather coat.
Her breasts yearn for marble.
The traffic halts: people fall out
of their cars. None of their most drooling
thoughts are wild enough
to build the ant-full crystal city
she would splinter with the tone of her step.

1963

Desperate sexual admirals
have captured Ste Catherine Street
In my naked pyjamas
I led them through the secret pass
Shelves of staircase people
feed their transistors
They have let the night into
their open shirts
three nipples at a time
And who lit that black star
with profound inflammable juices
and tuned my backbone
to a high wire moan
And listen everybody
just whose side am I on
Steered by the sticky dreams
of hairsome cabinboys
the boats slip through the rosejam night
into houses into white beds
Helen will leave her family tonight
She will climb away
for the sake of love only
My backbone whines like a siren
but nobody moves
The black star has sunk its spokes
it controls us like a sail
Lifetime staircase people
we're drifting together
There's nothing in store
for the doomed armada of wooden steps
steaming in the sweet black fire
of her guilt her promises
her royal raw impatience

July, 1964

32

Nancy lies in London grass
and George in Marco Polo's Pass
Leonard hasn't been the same
since he wandered from his name
Michael slowly dips his toe
in bathtubs filled with Turkish snow
Robert always loves to tell
how he became invisible
And all my friends are fast asleep
in places that are high and steep
their bodies torn on crosses
that their visions meant to leap
And in between their dreams they hate
the company they keep

1966

You broke the thin highway
where I drove drunk
in a souped-up tank
broke it
with your iron hairpin

Do you ever wonder
what these forests
are doing under my wheels

Crash crash the trees
sing as they fall
scraping against each other
like the hairy legs of crickets

Where was I going when
you snapped it
like a thread in mother's teeth
I'll never know

Crash crash sing the trees
What a big forest
What a great tank
What strange pieces of a highway
snarled in my treads

1963

Two went to sleep
almost every night
one dreamed of mud
one dreamed of Asia
visiting a zeppelin
visiting Nijinsky
Two went to sleep
one dreamed of ribs
one dreamed of senators
Two went to sleep
two travellers
The long marriage
in the dark
The sleep was old
the travellers were old
one dreamed of oranges
one dreamed of Carthage
Two friends asleep
years locked in travel
Goodnight my darling
as the dreams waved goodbye
one travelled lightly
one walked through water
visiting a chessgame
visiting a booth
always returning
to wait out the day
One carried matches
one climbed a beehive
one sold an earphone
one shot a German

Two went to sleep
every sleep went together
wandering away
from an operating table
one dreamed of grass
one dreamed of spokes
one bargained nicely
one was a snowman
one counted medicine
one tasted pencils
one was a child
one was a traitor
visiting heavy industry
visiting the family
Two went to sleep
none could foretell
one went with baskets
one took a ledger
one night happy
one night in terror
Love could not bind them
Fear could not either
they went unconnected
they never knew where
always returning
to wait out the day
parting with kissing
parting with yawns
visiting Death til
they wore out their welcome
visiting Death til
the right disguise worked
1964

What did I do with my breath
before your lies appointed me
detective of love?
Did I smell wine in little restaurants?
Did I bend over gardens?
Did I know where I was?
How many times did one of my friends
fall asleep his lips bright
with your slippery perfume?
Tell me how many times exactly
or I can't catch my breath.

Did I used to open the window
and think about the lilacs?
Did I detect hot-dogs
on St Lawrence Boulevard?
Did I like books?
Did I have a career?
How many times in what holes
exactly did you unfurl his
swimming flag of tiny stars?
I want to catch my breath
I want my old hay fever.

Did I have leisure time
before I started to reconstruct
every one of your nights?
Did I yawn?
Did I take walks without
looking for bodies?
Did I believe conversation?
Was music as necessary?
Did I love Euclid?
Was the air big?
Did I like surprises?

What did I do with my life before
your lies leaked the legend
of the fountain of s - - t
which I had to see for myself?
Did I sleep much?
Was there a menu tomorrow?
Did we have a dog?
Were horror movies fun?
Was I a freedom-rider
was I approximately a socialist
was I a prince in Canada
in the days before I followed
you and one of my friends?

Exactly where did you feel nothing?
Where are his eyes continuing?
How does it all continue?
Are reasons nice?
Is there any air in
the observation tower?
Does time fumigate?
Does detective of love
resign ever is detective bribed
with a huge sunset?
Are there lies which don't waste?
What did I do often in
the orchard with your name and
a great bouquet of raw pencils?
                                    July 12, 1964

I met Doc Dog The Poker Hound
in a clean cafeteria
All the farms of the country
were dark at that hour
I thought of wood and sleeping people
as we slurped the coffee
      What with the tile and neon
it was like some sidewalk cafe at noon
in a European capital city
      Doc Dog saw my face get sloppy
with a few old recollections
of farmhouses and foreign cities
being the traveller that I am
and he said
      One of these days
I'm going to open up a cafeteria
that serves coffee in thin cups
bone thin China cups
What we lose in cups we make up
in gratitude
      You have a big mouth you Poker Hound
Where the hell are you
I've been here for twenty years
and I never heard of you again
or your famous cafeteria

Found once again shamelessly ignoring the swans who inflame the spectators on the shores of American rivers; found once again allowing the juicy contract to expire because the telephone has a magic correspondence with my tapeworm; found once again leaving the garlanded manhood in danger of long official repose while it is groomed for marble in seedily historic back rooms; found once again humiliating the bank clerk with eye-to-eye wrestling, art dogma, lives that loaf and stare, and other stage whispers of genius; found once again the chosen object of heavenly longing such as can ambush a hermit in a forest with visions of a busy parking lot; found once again smelling mothball sweaters, titling home movies, untangling Victorian salmon rods, fanatically convinced that a world of sporty order is just around the corner; found once again planning the ideal lonely year which waits like first flesh love on a calendar of third choices; found once again hovering like a twine-eating kite over hands that feed me, verbose under the influence of astrology; found once again selling out to accessible local purity while Pentagon Tiffany evil alone can guarantee my power; found once again trusting that my friends grew up in Eden and will not harm me when at last I am armourless and absolutely silent; found once again at the very beginning, veteran of several useless ordeals, prophetic but not seminal, the purist for the masses of tomorrow; found once again sweetening life which I have abandoned, like a fired zoo-keeper sneaking peanuts to publicized sodomized elephants; found once again flaunting the rainbow which demonstrates that I am permitted only that which I urgently need; found once again cleansing my tongue of all possibilities, of all possibilities but my perfect one.

1964

The stars turn their noble stories,
turn their heroes upside-down;
the moon, obsessed calm moth
pursues its private candle past the dawn—

All these marvels happen
while I keep silent on my love
and say nothing for her beauty.

How can I use the gull's perfect orbit
round and round the hidden fish,
is there something to do as the sun
seizes and hardens the ridge of rocks?

Distant face, like an icon's
disciplined to tenderness,
my silence, it is for you?
May I survey the emptiness
that serves as field for the complete embrace?

1960

When I hear you sing
Solomon
animal throat, eyes beaming
sex and wisdom
My hands ache from

I left blood on the doors of my home
Solomon
I am very alone from aiming songs
at God for
I thought that beside me there was no one
Solomon

My secret fell on a language
It might have fallen like rust
on a tractor
It might have fallen on a trip
like manna
It fell like a drunk
into an elephant trap
Some of the spikes whispered:
        Secrets do not bleed
Some of the spikes whispered:
        Secrets which do not bleed
        are selfish.

1964

A goldfish died in a cloudy bowl
which I left on the pulpit while I —
never mind: my absence was not
justified.
     Belly up, soggy as wet
Kleenex, the wrong fins soft.
     Greed purifies in the way
it burns the world,
balancing wish with loss until
we own nothing but our perfect longing.
     The Fish Strikes Again
with its tiny crosses,
its misty sperm ocean past.

1964

O God as I called you before
when I was my father's father
It is thy world again
O God you are a souvenir of Lourdes
I am not ashamed to be a tourist
in the milky world
You are a plastic seashell
in which I hear a honeymoon
I am a souvenir of creation
You sank like a fish hook
through the layered mirrors of self love
O god change your name in my heart

Buy me buy me cries
the April sun bomb
Buy me cries the wind coming
in uneven kisses as the white summer
wears it to shreds
And me and me cry the khaki lovers
who saunter by in a game of shove and trip
You send me away with a vision of tunnels
that I can shake for snow and all aboard
Come back by a longer route
the thousand year dash
You beg me hoarsely
in a voice that sounds too much like books
      Child rest
and that is a souvenir
of where you will not call me back from
1965

Here was the Harbour, crowded with white ships, the gulls showing how much silver there was in the sunlight as they fell out of the sky like handfuls of polished rice, or climbed in smoky squadrons at the sun until their wings turned silver and they descended again to astonish the floating garbage.

Who doesn't give his heart to things that soar, kites or jet planes or a sharp distant sail? I tried to give more than my heart, I tried to yield my loathing, my ambition, all my tiny sicknesses, I tried to give away a new desire which I had hardly suspected but which was growing violently in the metal sunlight, like a germ culture suddenly surrounded by its own ideal conditions.

The gulls continued their cold acrobatics and refused to bear the smudges of my uneasiness. I think that more than hunger the sky was their master, they performed for the endless blue sky, confetti for some vast ceremony, an eternal wedding.

Give what you want to the gulls, the sky is not satisfied with the smudges of your character. It demands stories; of men the sky demands all manner of stories, entertainments, embroideries, just as it does of its stars and constellations. The sky does not care for this trait or that affliction, it wants the whole man lost in his story, abandoned in the mechanics of action, touching his fellows, leaving them, hunting the steps, dancing the old circles. The sky wants diagrams of our lives, it stores them like little curious wrist-watches, they are our wedding gifts.

He was lame
as a 3 legged dog
screamed as he came
through the fog

If you are the Light
give me a light
buddy

1965

I am too loud when you are gone
I am John the Baptist, cheated by mere water
and merciful love, wild but over-known
John of honey, of time, longing not for
music, longing, longing to be Him
I am diminished, I peddle versions of Word
that don't survive the tablets broken stone
I am alone when you are gone

1963

You know where I have been
Why my knees are raw
I'd like to speak to you
Who will see what I saw

Some men who saw me fall
Spread the news of failure
I want to speak to them
The dogs of literature

Pass me as I proudly
Passed the others
Who kneel in secret flight
Pass us proudly Brothers

Somewhere in my trophy room the crucifixion and other sacrifices were still going on, but the flesh and nails were grown over with rust and I could not tell where the flesh ended and the wood began or on which wall the instruments were hung.

I passed by limbs and faces arranged in this museum like hanging kitchen tools, and some brushed my arm as the hallway reeled me in, but I pocketed my hands along with some vulnerable smiles, and I continued on.

I heard the rooms behind me clamour an instant for my brain, and once the brain responded, out of habit, weakly, as if thinking someone else's history, and somewhere in that last tune it learned that it was not the Queen, it was a drone.

There ahead of me extended an impossible trophy: the bright, great sky, where no men lived. Beautiful and empty, now luminous with a splendour emanating from my own flesh, the tuneless sky washed and washed my lineless face and bathed in waves my heart like a red translucent stone. Until my eyes gave out I lived there as my home.

Today I know the only distance that I came was to the threshold of my trophy room. Among the killing instruments again I am further from sacrifice than when I began. I do not stare or plead with passing pilgrims to help me there. I call it discipline but perhaps it is fallen pride alone.

I'm not the one to learn an exercise for dwelling in the sky. My trophy room is vast and hung with crutches, ladders, braces, hooks. Unlike the invalid's cathedral, men hang with these instruments. A dancing wall of molecules, changing nothing, has cleared a place for me and my time.

1959, 1966

49

I guess it's time to say goodbye to all the secret clubs I wanted to command, it's time to end the signature I stretched from line to line. Come here, darling, I want to read your little hand. If it's all right to love you still I'd really like to see the sign.

That's a man, they said, a man we'll have to see
when we're ready to raise the final infantry

I told you where I've been and what I've lost and why. When I start to talk about my soul you always seem to smile and you ask if I got enough of the blanket that you made me buy and I don't know who's got who figured out as we plunge in ancient whispers down some river like the Nile.

I studied the departures of some fancy air-o-planes, I walked the airport corridors and I broke into a run. The signals that I scratched for you on frosty windowpanes, they melted when I barely missed the sun.

You saw me once too often climbing down the stairs that lead from the lip of your pedestal. I don't like the way I look from behind, and I wish you'd turn your marble head every time I fall. You said you wanted me naked so I hung my skin in the wind. Ah, the whole world felt so new. I didn't think when I tiptoed up those stairs that you'd treat me like a piece of meat on your barbeque.

That's a man, they said, a man we'll have to see
when we're ready to raise the final infantry.

For a long while I have been watching the city
push its fiery bones and organs through
the immense fluoroscope of night.
The King's yacht, like a swallowed brooch,
gleams digested in the fjord;
the harbour concentrates its light
like the result of a luminous internal test.
       Where is the disease I was so sure about?
Where apply the ruthless amputations I had planned?
The organism thrives, the skeleton lives,
has never lost its youth.
The notion of decay is my own secretion
which I stretch on every view
like the network of windows in spit.
       An airliner's lights blink over the moon,
soft as the footprints of a man moving in thought or devotion.
Is there work for every mind?
Lead me, technical fire, into families, cities, congregations:
I want to stroll down the arteries invisible
as the multitudes I cannot see from here.

Oslo, 1961

51

I was standing on the stairs
in the middle of the night,
the wind was filled with silver
the moon was out of sight.

And maybe I was waiting
but I knew you wouldn't come,
the night was soft as ashes
that a moth leaves on your thumb.

My birthday travelled through me
like a thread goes through a bead,
when it frayed and parted
I floated like a seed.

I was standing on the stairs
in the middle of the night,
the dandelions were yellow
the dandelions were white.

And are you really lucky
and are you really hexed
and how does love distract you
from one moment to the next?

I waited all the morning
and all the afternoon,
my flower it is the dandelion
my window is the moon.

Snow is falling.
There is a nude in my room.
She surveys the wine-coloured carpet.

She is eighteen.
She has straight hair.
She speaks no Montreal language.

She doesn't feel like sitting down.
She shows no gooseflesh.
We can hear the storm.

She is lighting a cigarette
from the gas range.
She holds back her long hair.

1958

Here was the Market, entering it was like turning over a dry stone and discovering a bright wet colony of worms, for me it was too soon to encounter the harbour's private parts, learning too soon the price of the feast. The structure was high and vast and somehow makeshift, sunlight poured through openings in the corrugated roof from a stained sun, not the same light outside, it must have been another sun with veins and suicide jugular, the light in the market was red and purple, before us stretched a corridor of meat, great torsos of meadow animals strung in glistening flayed exhibitions, heads with limp exhausted comic-book tongues dangling at too sharp an angle, heads with dull-eyed slaughter-greeting looks, heads smiling and winking, perhaps the subtlest camouflage this severed coyness, heads piled in pyramids like park cannonballs, some of them cruelly facing a sausage display of their missing extremities, a thick and thin suspended rain of sausages, a storm of jellied blood, and further down the corridor no recognizable animal shapes but chunks of their bodies, shaped not by hide or muscle but by cleaver, knife and appetite. It was damp in there, the air itself had a different texture from the outside, here it was some transluscent matter, and what was in the trash barrels was too small and hairy for this requiem, the smell had hands to keep you back, you breathed through your mouth. The men who sold and hosed the hanging meat were wet and bloody, painted like meat themselves, they seemed not so much vendors as kapos, prison trustees, favourites of the slaughter house who had been spared for their capacity to work, and they had a hundred sweets to bark at us as we moved in the crowd but not part of the crowd, down the corridor between the dripping walls, the staring fortresses, watching out for the black puddles underfoot, for who knows how deep they went.

I am anointed with directions
Trees and ships
see me stagger
like a fish in a shock of underwater dynamite
Blessed by the end of the world
I spin without wobbling
among the weathervanes
which hover like homeless helicopters
over the endless landing feast

1964

I met a woman long ago,
hair black as black can go.
Are you a teacher of the heart?
Soft she answered No.

I met a girl across the sea,
hair the gold that gold can be.
Are you a teacher of the heart?
Yes, but not for thee.

I knew a man who lost his mind
in some lost place I wished to find.
Follow me, he said,
but he walked behind.

I walked into a hospital
Where none was sick and none was well.
When at night the nurses left,
I could not walk at all.

Not too slow, not too soon
morning came, then came noon.
Dinner time a scalpel blade
lay beside my spoon.

Some girls wander by mistake
into the mess that scalpels make.
Are you teachers of the heart?
We teach old hearts to break.

One day I woke up alone,
hospital and nurses gone.
Have I carved enough?
You are a bone.

I ate and ate and ate,
I didn't miss a plate.
How much do these suppers cost?
We'll take it out in hate.

I spent my hatred everyplace,
on every work, on every face.
Someone gave me wishes.
I wished for an embrace.

Several girls embraced me, then
I was embraced by men.
Is my passion perfect?
Do it once again.

I was handsome, I was strong,
I knew the words of every song.
Did my singing please you?
The words you sang were wrong.

Who are you whom I address?
Who takes down what I confess?
Are you a teacher of the heart?
A chorus answered Yes.

Teachers, are my lessons done,
or must I do another one?
They laughed and laughed:
Child, you've just begun.

1965

You are The Model. This is how you walk home, leaving once and for all the table of minor American Buddhists in the Aegean who are very sweet but who will keep you back. Excuse yourself, leave the port, the kindly foreign colony, they are not the world, visit them someday on a yacht and remember names. Now in the darker town, star ache through the wide screen blue, the girl beside Vadim in a Paris rumour, solemn child body with surprising breasts in *Elle* net bathing suits, career in fashion elegance must must end in real power movies. Not if you stay with people who want so little, thin 19 blond, tipping moon foam off your white canvas thighs, get home and think, homesick, it's a beautiful night, penknife carved initials done out of love for you, where somewhere in the huge blue horoscope, is it a mistake, are you ordinary? Thin fame driven deer Vadim maybe new blond generation, stretchy sweater of tight pressed moons invisible bra moon nipple haze, 19, five years to do it. Walking home without autograph disciples for the last time, the last time that's a promise God, climbing white moon blunted steps, the Greeks are asleep and poor, unfashionable Greek island fine for little Buddhist kings. Smile for Vadim spies possibly scouting you out of the sparkling vast astrology right now, threaten Paris, threaten Jean Shrimpton, sleep with Vadim don't do everything the first time or do maybe, O God the night is so soft and beautiful, climb to the freshly made hotel, knowing how you look from behind, lemon scented sweater, long angles of leg lost unphotograph, homesick, 19, lying down, sometimes you have to be alone to be alone, saying prayers naked carefully, remembering every name, that's why you won't be punished, is Vadim on the way down, can any girl be discovered after Bardot?

1965

I've seen some lonely history
The heart cannot explore
I've scratched some empty blackboards
They have no teachers for

I trailed my meagre demons
From Jerusalem to Rome
I had an invitation
But the host was not at home

There were contagious armies
That spread their uniform
To all parts of my body
Except where I was warm

And so I wore a helmet
With a secret neon sign
That lit up all the boundaries
So I could toe the line

My boots got very tired
Like a sentry's never should
I was walking on a tightrope
That was buried in the mud

Standing at the drugstore
It was very hard to learn
Though my name was everywhere
I had to wait my turn

I'm standing here before you
I don't know what I bring
If you can hear the music
Why don't you help me sing

No disease or age makes the flesh unwind
but some strange unity of flesh and mind.
Your body's like those ships men must empty
of gold and oil to ride an unweaned sea,
boat of rib and skin, nothing that can bleed
or seas can suck or even death could need,
proving through the stark holds you bear and bring
that the voyage itself was everything.

1962

These notebooks, these notebooks!
Poetry is no substitute for survival.
In the books beside my bed
I used up my will like an alphabet.

Something mechanical and obsolete
is sawing up my heart with the blades
of those invisible wheels which kept
our grandfathers' airplanes aloft.

Is it a god who punishes,
is it a woman who pleases?
I admire riders of the immaculate molecule,
I crash in a heavy machine.

Arrogant as a farmer who won't
follow his children into the slums,
sometimes I believe I alone colonize
the sky with a handful of seeds.

I don't like the price of a belief.
Every god is jealous.
I am no parliamentarian
and there are no favourites of the Queen.

1966

Created fires I cannot love
lest I lose the ones above.
Poor enough, then I'll learn
to choose the fires where they burn.   .

O God, make me poor enough
to love your diamond in the rough,
or in my failure let me see
my greed raised to mystery.

Do you hate the ones who must
turn your world all to dust?
Do you hate the ones who ask
if Creation wears a mask?

God beyond the God I name,
if mask and fire are the same,
repair the seam my love leaps through,
uncreated fire to pursue.

Network of created fire,
maim my love and my desire.
Make me poor so I may be
servant in the world I see,

Or, as my love leaps wide,
confirm your servant in his pride:
if my love can't burn,
forbid a sickening return.

Is it here my love will train
not to leap so high again?
No praise here? no blame?
From my love you tear my name.

Unmake me as I'm washed
far from the fiery mask.
Gather my pride in the coded pain
which is also your domain.

Claim me, blood, if you have a story
to tell with my Jewish face,
you are strong and holy still, only
speak, like the Zohar, of a carved-out place
into which I must pour myself like wine,
an emptiness of history which I must seize
and occupy, calm and full in this confine,
becoming clear 'like good wine on its lees.'
1965

When a world is being born
all men labour at the birth
except the few here and there
who laboured long before.

At last they taste water
out of stones they broke,
honey from their bees
that yesterday were wild.

Honour them, but honour more
the early rarer labourers
who let their hunger wander
among ten million minds.

O love, we are not fed
with courage or with bread.
Commandeer my hunger
for the borning world

1965

He was beautiful when he sat alone, he was like me, he had wide lapels, he was holding the mug in the hardest possible way so that his fingers were all twisted but still long and beautiful, he didn't like to sit alone all the time, but this time, I swear, he didn't care one way or the other.

I'll tell you why I like to sit alone, because I'm a sadist, that's why we like to sit alone, because we're the sadists who like to sit alone.

He sat alone because he was beautifully dressed for the occasion and because he was not a civilian.

We are the sadists you don't have to worry about, you think, and we have no opinion on the matter of whether you have to worry about us, and we don't even like to think about the matter because it baffles us.

Maybe he doesn't mean a thing to me anymore but I think he was like me.

You didn't expect to fall in love, I said to myself and at the same time I answered gently, Do you think so?

I heard you humming beautifully, your hum said that I can't ignore you, that I'd finally come around for a number of delicious reasons that only you knew about, and here I am, Miss Blood.

And you won't come back, you won't come back to where you left me, and that's why you keep my number, so you don't dial it by mistake when you're fooling with the dial not even dialing numbers.

You begin to bore us with your pain and we have decided to change your pain.

You said you were happiest when you danced, you said you were happiest when you danced with me, now which do you mean?

And so we changed his pain, we threw the idea of a body at him and we told him a joke, and then he thought a great deal about laughing and about the code.

And he thought that she thought that he thought that she thought that the worst thing a woman could do was to take a man away from his work because that made her what, ugly or beautiful?

And now you have entered the mathematical section of your soul which you claimed you never had. I suppose that this, plus the broken heart, makes you believe that now you have a perfect right to go out and tame the sadists.

He had the last line of each verse of the song but he didn't have any of the other lines, the last line was always the same, *Don't call yourself a secret unless you mean to keep it.*

He thought he knew, or he actually did know too much about singing to be a singer; and if there actually is such a condition, is anybody in it, and are sadists born there?

It is not a question mark, it is not an exclamation point, it is a full stop by the man who wrote Parasites of Heaven.

Even if we stated our case very clearly and all those who held as we do came to our side, all of them, we would still be very few.

1966

I am a priest of God
I walk down the road
with my pockets in my hand
Sometimes I'm bad
then sometimes I'm very good
I believe that I believe
everything I should
I like to hear you say
when you dance with head rolling
upon a silver tray
that I am a priest of God

I though I was doing 100 other things
but I was a priest of God
I loved 100 women
never told the same lie twice
I said O Christ you're selfish
but I shared my bread and rice
I heard my voice tell the crowd
that I was alone and a priest of God
making me so empty
that even now in 1966
I'm not sure I'm a priest of God

In almond trees lemon trees
wind and sun do as they please
Butterflies and laundry flutter
My love her hair is blonde as butter

Wasps with yellow whiskers wait
for food beside her china plate
Ants beside her little feet
are there to share what she will eat

Who chopped down the bells that say
the world is born again today
We will feed you all my dears
this morning or in later years

Suzanne takes you down
to her place near the river,
you can hear the boats go by
you can stay the night beside her.
And you know that she's half crazy
but that's why you want to be there
and she feeds you tea and oranges
that come all the way from China.
Just when you mean to tell her
that you have no gifts to give her,
she gets you on her wave-length
and she lets the river answer
that you've always been her lover.

> And you want to travel with her,
> you want to travel blind
> and you know that she can trust you
> because you've touched her perfect body
> with your mind

Jesus was a sailor
when he walked upon the water
and he spent a long time watching
from a lonely wooden tower
and when he knew for certain
only drowning men could see him
he said All men will be sailors then
until the sea shall free them,
but he himself was broken
long before the sky would open,
forsaken, almost human,
he sank beneath your wisdom like a stone.

And you want to travel with him,
you want to travel blind
and you think maybe you'll trust him
because he touched your perfect body
with his mind.

Suzanne takes your hand
and she leads you to the river,
she is wearing rags and feathers
from Salvation Army counters.
The sun pours down like honey
on our lady of the harbour
as she shows you where to look
among the garbage and the flowers,
there are heroes in the seaweed
there are children in the morning,
they are leaning out for love
they will lean that way forever
while Suzanne she holds the mirror.
And you want to travel with her
and you want to travel blind
and you're sure that she can find you
because she's touched her perfect body
with her mind.

Give me back my fingerprints
My fingertips are raw
If I don't get my fingerprints
I have to call the Law

I touched you once too often
& I don't know who I am
My fingerprints were missing
When I wiped away the jam

I called my fingerprints all night
But they don't seem to care
The last time that I saw them
They were leafing thru your hair

I thought I'd leave this morning
So I emptied out your drawer
A hundred thousand fingerprints
Floated to the floor

You hardly stooped to pick them up
You don't count what you lose
You don't even seem to know
Whose fingerprints are whose

When I had to say goodbye
You weren't there to find
You took my fingerprints away
So I would love your mind

I don't pretend to understand
Just what you mean by that
But nextime I'll inquire
Before I scratch your back

I wonder if my fingerprints
Get lonely in the crowd
There are no others like them
& that should make them proud

Now you want to marry me
& take me down the aisle
& throw confetti fingerprints
You know that's not my style

Sure I'd like to marry
But I won't face the dawn
With any girl who knew me
When my fingerprints were on
1966

Foreign God, reigning in earthly glory between the Godless God and this greedy telescope of mine: touch my hidden jelly muscle, ring me with some power, I must conquer Babylon and New York. Draw me with a valuable sign, raise me to your height. You and I, dear Foreign God, we both are demons who must disappear in the perpetual crawling light, the fumbling sparks printing the shape of each tired form. We must be lost soon in the elementary kodak experiment, in the paltry glory beyond our glory, the chalksqueak of our most limitless delight. We are devoted yokels of the mothy parachute, the salvation of ordeal, we paid good money for the perfect holy scab, the pilgrim kneecap, the shoulder freakish under burden, the triumphant snowman who does not freeze. Down with your angels, Foreign God, down with us, adepts of magic: into the muddy fire of our furthest passionate park, let us consign our-selves now, puddles, peep-holes, dreary oceanic pomp seen through the right end of the telescope, the minor burn, the kingsize cigarette, the alibi atomic holocaust, let us consign ourselves to the unmeasured exile outside the rules of law-lessness. O God, in thy foreign or godless form, in thy form of illusion or with the ringscape of your lethal thumb, you stop direction, you crush this down, you abandon the evidence you pressed on its tongue.

1965

This morning I was dressed by the wind.
The sky said, close your eyes and run
this happy face into a sundrift.
The forest said, never mind, I am as old
as an emerald, walk into me gossiping.
The village said, I am perfect and intricate,
would you like to start right away?
My darling said, I am washing my hair in the water
we caught last year, it tastes of stone.
This morning I was dressed by the wind,
it was the middle of September in 1965.

I believe you heard your master sing
while I lay sick in bed
I believe he told you everything
I keep locked in my head
Your master took you traveling
at least that's what you said
O love did you come back to bring
your prisoner wine and bread

You met him at a nightclub where
they take your clothes at the door
He was just a numberless man of a pair
who has just come back from the war
You wrap his quiet face in your hair
and he hands you the apple core
and he touches your mouth now so suddenly bare
of the kisses you had on before

He gave you a German Shepherd to walk
with a collar of leather and nails
He never once made you explain or talk
about all of the little details
such as who had a worm and who had a rock
and who had you through the mails
Your love is a secret all over the block
and it never stops when he fails

He took you on his air-o-plane
which he flew without any hands
and you cruised above the ribbons of rain
that drove the crowd from the stands
Then he killed the lights on a lonely lane
where an ape with angel glands
erased the final wisps of pain
with the music of rubber bands

And now I hear your master sing
You pray for him to come
His body is a golden string
that your body is hanging from
His body is a golden string
My body is growing numb
O love I hear your master sing
Your shirt is all undone

Will you kneel beside the bed
we polished long ago
before your master chose instead
to make my bed of snow
Your hair is wild your knuckles red
and you're speaking much too low
I can't make out what your master said
before he made you go

I think you're playing far too rough
For a lady who's been to the moon
I've lain by the window long enough
(you get used to an empty room)
Your love is some dust in an old man's cuff
who is tapping his foot to a tune
and your thighs are a ruin and you want too much
Let's say you came back too soon

I loved your master perfectly
I taught him all he knew
He was starving in a mystery
like a man who is sure what is true
I sent you to him with my guarantee
I could teach him something new
I taught him how you would long for me
No matter what he said no matter what you do

77

I stepped into an avalanche
It covered up my soul
When I am not a hunchback
I sleep beneath a hill
You who wish to conquer pain
Must learn to serve me well

You strike my side by accident
As you go down for gold
The cripple that you clothe and feed
is neither starved nor cold
I do not beg for company
in the centre of the world

When I am on a pedestal
you did not raise me there
your laws do not compel me
to kneel grotesque and bare
I myself am pedestal
for the thing at which you stare

You who wish to conquer pain
must learn what makes me kind
The crumbs of love you offer me
are the crumbs I've left behind
Your pain is no credential
It is the shadow of my wound

I have begun to claim you
I who have no greed
I have begun to long for you
I who have no need
The avalanche you're knocking at
is uninhabited

Do not dress in rags for me
I know you are not poor
Don't love me so fiercely
when you know you are not sure
It is your world beloved
It is your flesh I wear

I see you on a Greek mattress, 30
I stepped into an avalanche, 78
It's not so hard to say goodbye, 12
I've seen some lonely history, 59
I was standing on the stairs, 52
I wonder if my brother will ever read this, 29
My secret fell on a language, 42
Nancy lies in London grass, 33
No disease or age makes the flesh unwind, 60
Nothing has been broken, 22
O God as I called you before, 44
O love intrude into this strangerhood, 25
One night I burned the house I loved, 18
Snow is falling, 53
Somewhere in my trophy room . . . , 49
So you're the kind of vegetarian, 11
Suzanne takes you down, 70
Suzanne wears a leather coat, 31
Terribly awake I wait, 28
The nightmares do not suddenly, 13
These notebooks, these notebooks, 61
The stars turn their noble stories, 40
This morning I was dressed by the wind, 75
Two went to sleep, 35
What did I do with my breath, 36
When a world is being born, 65
When I hear you sing, 41
When I paid the sun to run, 24
You are the Model, 58
You broke the thin highway, 34
You know there was honey in my system, 20
You know where I have been, 48